W9-AGF-813

DATE DUE		

DISCARD

TEMPERATE DECIDUOUS FORESTS

Lands of Falling Leaves

by Laura Purdie Salas

illustrated by Jeff Yesh

Thanks to our advisers for their expertise, research, and advice:

Michael T. Lares, Ph.D., Associate Professor of Biology
University of Mary, Bismarck, North Dakota

Susan Kesselring, M.A., Literacy Educator
Rosemount–Apple Valley–Eagan (Minnesota) School District

PICTURE WINDOW BOOKS
Minneapolis, Minnesota

Editor: Jill Kalz

Designers: Joe Anderson and Hilary Wacholz

Page Production: Melissa Kes

Art Director: Nathan Gassman

Associate Managing Editor: Christianne Jones

The illustrations in this book were created digitally.

Picture Window Books

5115 Excelsior Boulevard

Suite 232

Minneapolis, MN 55416

877-845-8392

www.picturewindowbooks.com

Printed in the United States of America.

Library of Congress Cataloging-in-Publication Data

Salas, Laura Purdie.

Temperate deciduous forests : lands of falling leaves / by Laura Purdie Salas ; illustrated by Jeff Yesh.

p. cm. — (Amazing science)

Includes bibliographical references and index.

ISBN-13: 978-1-4048-3099-8 (library binding)

ISBN-10: 1-4048-3099-5 (library binding)

ISBN-13: 978-1-4048-3473-6 (paperback)

ISBN-10: 1-4048-3473-7 (paperback)

1. Forest animals—Juvenile literature. 2. Forest plants—Juvenile literature.

3. Forests and forestry—Juvenile literature I. Yesh, Jeff, 1971- II. Title.

QH86.S243 2006

577.3–dc22   2006027217

Table of Contents

Falling Leaves

Dry leaves crackle underfoot. Sun shines through the bare tree branches. Chipmunks and squirrels store nuts in hollow logs. This is the end of autumn in the temperate deciduous forest ecosystem. An ecosystem is all of the living and nonliving things in a certain area. It includes plants, animals, water, soil, weather … everything!

FUN FACT

The word *deciduous* means "falling down." Every autumn, the leaves of deciduous trees fall to the ground. If the trees didn't drop their leaves, they would dry out during the winter and die.

Where Forests Grow

North America

South America

Temperate deciduous forests cover much of the eastern United States. They also grow in Europe and Asia.

Deciduous forests are common where there is a lot of rain or snow. Temperatures range from below freezing to 80 degrees Fahrenheit (27 degrees Celsius) or more. Forests need at least four months of warm weather each year to grow.

TEMPERATE DECIDUOUS FORESTS

Europe

Asia

Africa

EQUATOR

Australia

FUN FACT

The word *temperate* means "not too hot and not too cold."
Temperatures in temperate deciduous forests generally stay
within a certain range. There may be periods of very hot or
very cold weather, but those periods don't last long.

Four Seasons

Each of the four seasons brings change to the temperate deciduous forests. Forest trees begin to grow leaves during the spring. By summer, most trees are full and green.

Spring

Summer

Then, autumn arrives. The days get shorter, and the air turns chilly. Most tree leaves turn color and drop to the ground. Snow often covers the bare deciduous trees in the winter.

Autumn

Winter

FUN FACT

Deciduous forests get more rain and snow than any other ecosystem except the rain forest. Between 30 and 60 inches (76 and 152 centimeters) of rain and melted snow soak into the ground every year.

Layers of the Forest

The temperate deciduous forest has four layers.

The tops of tall trees make the canopy. The canopy is the roof of the forest. It sits about 90 feet (27 meters) above the ground.

Smaller trees and young trees make up the second layer, called the understory.

The next layer is the forest floor. Shrubs, ferns, and dead trees make up this layer.

Soil is the bottom layer. Forest soil has tiny bits of plant and animal matter in it, called humus. Humus makes the soil rich and helps plants and trees grow.

canopy

understory

FUN FACT

Sun-loving trees such as oak, walnut, and elm form the canopy.
They block the sun and shade the rest of the forest. The plants
and trees below the canopy must be able to grow in shade.

forest floor

soil

Soaking Up the Sun

Maple, hickory, and oak trees are common temperate deciduous forest trees. They all have broad, flat leaves. The leaves can soak up lots of sun. Trees need sun to make food for themselves.

Maple

Hickory

FUN FACT

Most deciduous leaves are really a mixture of colors. In the spring and summer, when trees are making a lot of food, the leaves are filled with green coloring. The green is very dark and hides the other colors. In autumn, when the trees stop making food, the green coloring breaks down. Then you can see the yellow and orange colors that were there all along.

Oak

Shade-Loving Plants

Small plants in a temperate deciduous forest don't get much sun in the summer and early autumn. Tall, leafy trees block most of it. So small plants that love shade grow well in forests. Ferns, mosses, and bluebells are common forest plants. They often get nutrients from the decaying wood of fallen trees, called nurse logs.

In the spring, more sun reaches the forest floor. That's because tree branches are not yet full of leaves. Dutchman's breeches and spring beauties are two wildflowers that bloom in early spring.

FUN FACT

Mushrooms live in deciduous forests, too. Mushrooms are a kind of fungus. A fungus looks like a plant in many ways, but it's not a plant. It cannot make its own food, like a plant does. It soaks up its food from the soil or from nearby plants.

Forest Animals

Animals of all shapes and sizes live in the temperate deciduous forest. The smallest include worms and bugs, mice and chipmunks, snakes and rabbits. Tree branches are filled with blue jays, woodpeckers, owls, and other birds.

Larger mammals such as deer, cougars, and black bears also live in the forest. So do amphibians such as frogs and salamanders.

FUN FACT

Forest animals such as snakes, ground squirrels, and black bears hibernate in the winter. They eat a lot of food, find a safe place, and sleep the winter away.

Forests in Danger

Temperate deciduous forests are strong, but people can do a lot of damage to them. Because the soil is rich in nutrients, people around the world have cut down forests to make room for farms. People also cut down trees to use the wood for fuel. Pollution from cars and factories poisons the air and water that forests need to survive.

Deer can harm forests, too. Many of the large animals that eat deer have been killed off. As a result, there are too many deer. They eat so many wildflowers that they can leave the forest floor bare.

Hardworking Forest

The temperate deciduous forest is an ecosystem full of gifts. It gives homes to many animals. The roots of its plants and trees stop soil from washing into rivers and polluting the water. The trees catch dust in the breeze and take carbon dioxide from the air. These things help clean the air.

It's important to protect the forest ecosystems and all of Earth's other ecosystems, too. Each has its own special gifts. Together, Earth's ecosystems make the planet an amazing place to live!

FUN FACT

Paper is also made from trees. Without trees, you wouldn't have this book to read. Most paper companies have planting programs to replace the trees they cut down.

Temperate Deciduous Forest Diorama: Forest in a Box

WHAT YOU NEED:

- a shoebox
- brown and blue paint
- a paintbrush
- self-drying modeling clay
- colored paper
- scissors
- glue
- pictures of forest animals, such as squirrels, rabbits, and deer

WHAT YOU DO:

1. First, turn the shoebox on its side.

2. Paint the inside of the box. The sides and bottom should be brown and the top blue.

3. Use self-drying modeling clay to make the tall forest tree trunks. Use colored paper to make the leafy canopy.

4. Include at least one smaller tree, a shrub, and some ground plants in the forest scene.

5. Use colored paper, clay, or pictures to make the forest animals.

6. Now, how would you change your forest diorama to make it look like winter? Which colors would you use? Which animals and plants would you add or take out?

Temperate Deciduous Forest Facts

- Sap begins to run inside maple trees on warm spring days. Sugar makers collect the sap and boil it down to make maple syrup. It takes 40 gallons (152 liters) of sap to make 1 gallon (3.8 L) of maple syrup.

- The American chestnut tree used to be common in the deciduous forest. In 1904, someone brought trees from another country to New York City. Those trees carried a disease called chestnut blight. The blight spread to the American chestnuts, and all of the large trees died.

- Skunk cabbage is a forest plant that forms its leaves underground during the fall. As spring nears, the skunk cabbage actually makes heat. The heat helps melt the snow and ground around the plant so the leaves can push upward. Skunk cabbage is one of the first forest plants to come above ground in the spring. The plant gets its name from the rotten smell it releases when its leaves are damaged.

Glossary

amphibians—cold-blooded animals with a backbone and moist skin that usually live in or near water

carbon dioxide—the waste gas that humans and animals breathe out

deciduous—dropping leaves every year

ecosystem—an area with certain animals, plants, weather, and land or water features

hibernate—to sleep deeply or rest during the winter

mammals—warm-blooded animals that feed their young milk

nutrients—parts of foods that are used for growth; vitamins are nutrients

temperate—not too hot and not too cold

To Learn More

AT THE LIBRARY

Galko, Francine. *Forest Animals*. Chicago: Heinemann Library, 2002.

Johnson, Rebecca L., and Phyllis V. Saroff. *A Walk in the Deciduous Forest*. Minneapolis: Carolrhoda Books, 2001.

Longenecker, Theresa. *Who Grows Up in the Forest?* Mankato, Minn.: Picture Window Books, 2003.

Wilkins, Sally. *Temperate Forests*. Mankato, Minn.: Bridgestone Books, 2001.

ON THE WEB

FactHound offers a safe, fun way to find Web sites related to this book. All of the sites on FactHound have been researched by our staff.

1. Visit *www.facthound.com*
2. Type in this special code: 1404830995
3. Click on the FETCH IT button.

Your trusty FactHound will fetch the best sites for you!

Index

LOOK FOR ALL OF THE BOOKS IN THE AMAZING SCIENCE–ECOSYSTEMS SERIES:

Deserts: Thirsty Wonderlands

Grasslands: Fields of Green and Gold

Oceans: Underwater Worlds

Rain Forests: Gardens of Green

Temperate Deciduous Forests: Lands of Falling Leaves

Wetlands: Soggy Habitat